Real Life Stories

WOMEN IN THE WEST

Jill Bryant

— Weigl Publishers Inc. —

About *Women in the West*
This book is based on the real life accounts of the people who settled the American West. History is brought to life through quotes from personal journals, letters to family back home, and historical records of those who traveled West to build a better life.

Published by Weigl Publishers Inc.
123 South Broad Street, Box 227
Mankato, MN 56002
USA

Web site: www.weigl.com

Library of Congress Cataloging-in-Publication Data

Bryant, Jill.
  Women in the West / by Jill Bryant.
    p. cm. -- (Real life stories series)
  Summary: Briefly explores what it was like for a woman to live and work in the Old West, including first-hand accounts about such things as making soap, clothing, and nutritious meals.
  Includes bibliographical references and index.
  ISBN 1-59036-083-4 (Library Bound : alk. paper)
  1. Women pioneers--West (U.S.)--History--19th century--Juvenile literature. 2. Pioneers--West (U.S.)--History--19th century--Juvenile literature. 3. Frontier and pioneer life--West (U.S.)--Juvenile literature. 4. West (U.S.)--History--19th century--Juvenile literature. 5. West (U.S.)--Social life and customs--19th century--Juvenile literature.   [1. Women pioneers.   2. Pioneers--West (U.S.) 3. Frontier and pioneer life--West   (U.S.) 4. West (U.S.)--History. 5. West (U.S.)--Social life and customs.] I. Title. II. Series.
  F596.B885 2003
  978'.02'082--dc21

                    2002012728

Printed in the United States of America
1 2 3 4 5 6 7 8 9 0   06 05 04 03 02

Photograph Credits
Cover: CORBIS/MAGMA; **Corbis Corporation:** page 21R; **Denver Public Library Western History Department:** pages 6 (Z-1172), 22 (X-21929); **Glenbow Archives:** pages 1 (NA-3836-1), 4 (NA-1742-8), 8 (NA-1941-12); **Fred Hultstrand History in Pictures Collections, Institute for Regional Studies & University Archives, North Dakota State University:** pages 5 (2028.108), 18 (2028.183); **photos courtesy Minnesota Pioneer Park:** pages 10, 14, 21L; **Photo 24:** pages 12/13 (13573-10043-24); **photo courtesey Stacey Johnson:** pages 3, 16.

Project Coordinator Michael Lowry	**Copy Editor** Frances Purslow	**Layout** Terry Paulhus
Substantive Editor Christa Bedry	**Design** Virginia Boulay & Bryan Pezzi	**Photo Research** Dylan Kirk & Daorcey Le Bray

Contents

Westward Bound!

Men and women of all ages wanted to travel to the **West**. Many people were in search of adventure and free land. Other **settlers** were following family members or friends. Half of the settlers traveling west in 1857 were women.

Most of the women that were traveling west were married. They traveled with their husbands and children. Some women traveled with family members. They wanted to live near their brothers, sisters, aunts, and uncles.

Women who traveled west often left behind a comfortable house, plenty of furniture, family, and friends.

Helping Hands

Members of the community kept each other company and helped each other survive in the harsh lands of the West. How do people in your community help you?

Her Own Home

Women ran the households. They cared for the children. They cooked the meals and washed the clothes. The women looked after vegetable gardens and **preserved** foods. They **churned** butter and made cheese. There was little time for rest. Many women were proud of their new homes. Most of the women were happy with their new lives in the West.

The women living in the West used the fresh fruits and vegetables from their gardens to make the family's food.

Real Life Stories

"[A]ny woman who can stand her own company, can see the beauty of the sunset, loves growing things, and is willing to put in as much time at careful labor as she does over the washtub, will certainly succeed; will have independence, plenty to eat all the time, and a home of her own in the end."

Elinore Pruitt Stewart

Home Cooking

The women baked their own bread. They ground corn, wheat, and oats into flour. The flour was used for baking. Corn was used in almost every meal in the Southwest. Beans, cabbages, carrots, peas, potatoes, pumpkins, onions, and turnips were common vegetables in the West.

The settlers ate ham, salted pork, and beef. Buffalo, birds, deer, fish, moose, and rabbits were also part of the settler's diet. Women salted or smoked meat over the fire to preserve it.

The women milked the dairy cows. They often looked after the sheep, chickens, and pigs on the farm.

Real Life Stories

"We had food which met the needs of growing bodies, and we did not have to keep a bottle of vitamins from A to Z to keep us in good health."

Myrtle Oxford Hersh

Family Fashions

It took the women a long time to make clothes. First, the women gathered **flax**. Next, they spun the flax on a spinning wheel to make yarn. A **loom** was used to weave the homespun yarn into cloth. Finally, the women sewed the clothes. Women made dresses, pants, and shirts.

Women in the West combined flax with wool from sheep to make a fabric called linsey-woolsey. This was a thick, warm cloth.

Real Life Stories

"We children were supplied with homespun clothing through the efforts of our devoted parents—especially our mother.
Spinning was one of the common household duties of the women and the loom was not less necessary in the cabin home than the wheel, and many women did their own weaving."

Mahala Blout Mills

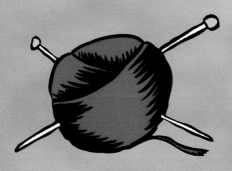

A Healthy Home

Most doctors lived far away. There was not a fast way to visit a doctor. The women took care of many health problems. Home **remedies** were passed from mother to daughter. Native Americans shared many natural remedies with the settlers. Remedies were made from common foods and herbs.

Settlers used teas made from nearby plants to treat many illnesses. They drank elderberry blossom tea to soothe a cold. Buttercup tea treated **asthma**. Chamomile tea settled an upset stomach.

Honey was used to soothe a sore throat. It was also spread on cuts to stop infection.

A paste of baking soda and water was used to soothe burns and bee stings.

Upset stomachs were calmed with water and vinegar.

Settlers ate white onions to help them sleep.

Wash Day

The women heated water over a fire on wash day. They scrubbed the wet clothes on a washboard. The soap they used was homemade. The women rinsed the clothes and wrung them out. The clothes were then hung to dry. The women ironed the clothes once they were dry. The irons were very heavy and had to be heated on the stove.

Doing the laundry was a huge chore. Luckily settlers had few clothes. What chores do you do at home?

Real Life Stories

"When the soap started to thicken, the kettle had to be watched very closely or it would boil over. When the soap had been cooked enough, it was stirred over and over again. It was beaten until it became white. The more it was beaten the more white the soap became."

Alice Lund

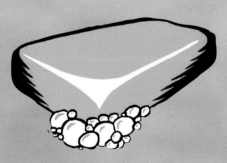

A Dollar Earned

Women living in the West sold eggs, butter, and honey. The money earned from these items helped the family survive tough times. Some women earned money outside the home. Young women often worked as schoolteachers. Other careers for women included nurses, **midwives**, **land speculators**, journalists, and cowgirls.

Some women became schoolteachers when they were only 14 years old.

Real Life Stories

"Mother took particular pains to see that all eggs were clean and fresh when sold or we didn't sell any. Butter was worked until every bit of moisture was out of it and it was near the same color at all times as possible, and the cream that went into its production was carefully tended. It wasn't long until the store had standing orders for her produce."

Percy Wollaston

Women Homesteaders

The Homestead Act was announced in 1862. It offered free land to men and women equally. Women came to the West from all over the world. They claimed and farmed their own land. They were known as women homesteaders. The promise of jobs as housekeepers and schoolteachers drew many women to the West. Women ran homesteads. Women worked outside of the house. Women in the West were the first to vote. These were exciting times.

Colorado and Wyoming both had many women homesteaders. About 20 percent of the people who claimed homesteads were women between 1887 and 1908.

The Highlights of Women Homesteading

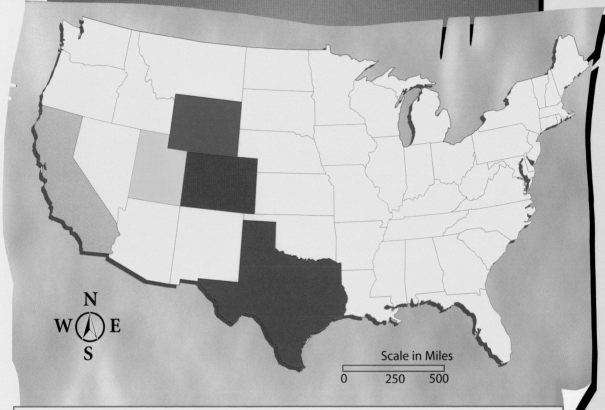

Scale in Miles
0   250   500

Key

■ Wyoming was the first state to allow women to vote. The first woman governor in the United States was elected in 1924. She was the governor of Wyoming.

■ The first three women to make laws in the United States were elected in Colorado in 1894.

■ Texas had many women homesteaders. About 1,481 women claimed land between 1845 and 1898.

■ California was home to a successful business woman. Mary Ellen Pleasant built laundries, cookhouses, and general stores throughout the state.

■ Utah had 17,000 women voters in 1870. This state had the largest number of woman voters at the time.

Learning More about Women in the West

To learn more about Women in the West, you can borrow books from the library or surf the Internet.

Books

Furbee, Mary Rodd. *Outrageous Women of the American Frontier.* New York: John Wiley & Sons, Inc., 2002.

Goodman, Susan E. *Ultimate Field Trip 4: A Week in the 1800s.* New York: Atheneum Books for Young Readers, 2000.

Web Sites

Frontier House
www.pbs.org/wnet/frontierhouse/
Experience life on the frontier at this Web site.

Encarta
www.encarta.com
Enter the search word "pioneer" into an online encyclopedia, such as Encarta.

Compare and Contrast

Borrow some books about settlers from the library. Look at the pictures. What did the women settlers wear during summer months? What did they wear to keep warm? Divide a piece of paper in half. Draw a picture of a woman settler on one side. On the other side, draw a woman from today. Use arrows to label the items of clothing. Research which items would have been homemade and which would have been bought from a store.

What Have You Learned?

Based on what you have just read, try to answer the following questions.

1

Which vegetable did settlers in the Southwest eat at almost every meal?

a) turnips
b) corn
c) peas
d) carrots

2

True or false? Spinning was one of the household duties of women.

3

What did women do to preserve meat?

a) froze it
b) cooked it
c) smoked it
d) fried it

4

What did women settlers use to soothe bee stings?

a) baking soda paste
b) honey
c) peanut butter
d) cow's milk

5

True or false? Linsey-woolsey was a type of food.

6

True or false? Women had to heat the water over a fire before washing the clothes.

23

Words to Know

asthma: a disease that results in difficulty in breathing

churned: stirred or shaken

flax: a type of plant that can be used to make yarn

land speculators: people who buy and resell land to make money

loom: a tool for weaving yarn or thread into cloth

midwives: someone trained to help women give birth

preserved: treated to prevent from spoiling

remedies: medicines to treat or cure an illness or relieve symptoms

settlers: people who set up their homes in a new region

West: region of the United States west of the Mississippi River

Index

24